Praise for *Blackout*

'*Blackout* offers an extended reflection on living within silence and emptiness, but through the accumulation of seemingly disconnected stories something else emerges: the pangs of absence enfolded one after another – but absence is always presence, silence is a teeming noise... Was the collective amnesia that followed our recent, yet somehow erased, enforced isolation necessary to forgetting a deeper revelation? For a moment, another kind of society presented itself, a society of gorgeous nothings given eyes to see in the dark.' – **David Toop**

'Silence is etymologically rooted in the idea of being quiet and still, of attending. The defining 'absence of sound' came much later. There are reasons why retreats are often predicated on silence. They seek to face directly the fear we have – identified so keenly by Jung – of the journey to the interior that 'silence' prompts. There is no such thing as absolute silence, of course. In an anechoic chamber, you become the sound you hear: your lungs, your heart, your eyelids. Tytelman's remarkable meditation on the presences made vivid by absence understands this instinctively, emotionally, intellectually and even metaphysically. He listens beyond listening. We carry our own silence and that of others like organs. We make our own silences and harvest them. In his haunted and haunting text, even ghosts are breathing.' – **Gareth Evans**

BLACKOUT

by

Yann Chateigné Tytelman

Translated from the French
by Clem Clement

LesFugitives

London

This first English-language edition published by Les Fugitives editions in the United Kingdom in October 2025 • Les Fugitives Ltd, 91 Cholmley Gardens, Fortune Green Road, London NW6 1UN • www.lesfugitives.com • English-language translation © Clem Clement, 2025 • First published as *Blackout* by Centre d'édition contemporaine Geneva © 2023 • Cover design by Claire Evrard • Cover illustration: Eclipse © Ann Veronica Janssens, 2017, from a video taken in Warm Spring by Rainbow Robotics/Rainbow Astro. Photograph from a projection at Galerie Micheline Szwajcer © Vildana Memic, courtesy of Mister Ho and Micheline Szwajcer • Text design by MacGuru Ltd • A CIP catalogue record for this book is available from the British Library • The rights of Yann Chateigné Tytelman to be identified as author, and the rights of Clem Clement to be identified as translator of this work have been identified in accordance with Section 77 of the Copyright, Designs and Patents Act 1988 • Printed in the EU • EU Authorised Representative: Easy Access System Europe - Mustamäetee 50, 10621 Tallinn, Estonia, gpsr.requests@easproject.com • ISBN: 978-1-0683001-5-8 •

PREFACE

'I wanted to write to you so I could talk to you about silence…' With this quiet invocation, Yann Chateigné Tytelman, a curator, editor and writer based in Brussels, opens *Blackout,* an elegant meditation on absence, memory, and the elusive nature of grief. What follows is not simply a book, but a constellation of reflections, a poetic and philosophical journey into the experience of a void and other layered moments of stillness.

'Recently I made a rule for myself: never to let a day pass without writing to someone who is, or once was, dear to me,' he writes. It is a clue to the gentle, consistent practice that underpins the narrative that is framed by two elements: an impulse to write to his father, ten years after his death, and undertaking a controlled, psychedelic 'trip' using the sacred herb *Salvia divinorum*.

The result cannot be presented in linear form. Instead, Tytelman's story is necessarily fragmented. Initially, the sections seem digressive, but the work quickly reveals itself as tightly composed, with each section essential, each image resonant and poignant. Together, they form a connective narrative tissue between the past and the present, between intimate memories and visceral encounters with artistic works and processes.

The silence Tytelman explores is not singular. It is layered: the death of a father, the rupture of daily life during lockdown, and quieter, more ambiguous stillnesses that shape his inner world. Cultural touchstones are wide-ranging, from Brian Eno's ambient music to John Cage's Thoreauvian silence, from Mieko Shiomi's *Water Music* to Charles Ray's *Ink Box*, reflections offered to the reader as he attempts to classify and understand silences and voids: their textures, their formlessness. Descriptions of artist Vija Celmins' oceanscapes, translated from photographs into different media, are particularly resonant, perhaps offering a visual model of composition to be replicated through text. When reflecting on Celmins' work, we have a feeling of senses merging: words carry sound. Images evoke touch, as Tytelman sensitively seeks to give shape to the 'images between the images, like the silences between notes.'

If this all sounds highly cerebral, in one way it is. However, each encounter is tethered to a lived experience. As I read, I felt increasingly connected to Tytelman's expression of tangible human experiences – loneliness, confinement, loss – and drawn steadily closer to the emotional core of the text: a renewed psychological understanding of his father. These insights enable him to forge an intimate, expressive shape for a son's lament: 'I wanted to save you, but I was the one who left.' Spoken to the ghost of a man whose life was shaped by labour, dust, and work. A sharp contrast to Tytelman's art-drift into a world of galleries and libraries; a painful severance. To engage with *Blackout* is to be intimately connected with Tytelman's emotional interiority, and it feels like embodied engagement, rather than an abstract process of reading, assisted by the fluid and delicate translation into English by Clem Clement. It is immensely moving.

Through depictions of photographs and recursive reflections, Tytelman's writing here evokes the grief-work of Roland Barthes and the mosaic-like narrative disruptions of Nathalie Léger's oeuvre. Yet his approach, shaped by art, psychedelia, and philosophical inquiry, is entirely his own. Drawing on Giorgio Agamben's idea that writing is not a fixed form, but an experience born of life itself, this book becomes more than a tribute. It is a haunting, delicately woven elegy; a luminous act of love written into the void. Let it draw you in. Let it speak to your own silences.

– Suzanne Joinson
August 2025

BLACKOUT

*

We woke one morning and the lands of our existence had slipped. Little by little, my brain has morphed into a new organ, one lacking the ability to retain certain information. I often have to make an effort to remind myself of times, dates, things to do, the people I have seen and the conversations we have had. It is strange how predictions can sometimes be disproven. I had believed in the threat of a future that, we had been told, would be based on total recall, on our inability to forget, on the modification of our personal memories, informed by every medium, everywhere, which serves us. Suddenly, the scene grows dark and I must remind myself several times that today, it is spring.

*

I wanted to write to you so I could talk to you about silence, about the unforeseeable silence which fell all at once over our neighbourhood. I feel as though I will never be able to escape it, even though we have already moved twice since then. Perhaps it is the silence itself which never leaves me, as if it were hanging on me like a halo, following me everywhere, clinging to my body, insinuated beneath my skin. I search for an answer but find none: what is this silence I speak of? When did it set in? Something began further back in the past. I realise that many things will no longer be as they were before, that they will take time – a long time – to change. Was it the isolation, the disease, or the omnipresent fear which brought me back to your absence? No, I remember. It was you, one day, who came back. Without a word, you appeared to me.

*

I close my eyes. I try to dissolve myself in time, to feel what happened. I perceive only flashes, sensations. I see lights, but everything is still blurry, fragmented. It is a little as though I had been in an accident, and at first had not felt the impact; then as though the shockwave were spreading, invisible and powerful, through all my limbs. At the same time, I realised that I was experiencing violence of another kind, emanating from other bodies; a violence experienced by other nervous systems just like mine, but whose proportional force rippled out to the unknown and profound limits of its propagation.

*

One day, I began to classify silences. I collected notes and clues. In their own way, they spoke to me. I realised that, strangely, there was neither sound nor music in this initial constellation, only images and words. Things that were themselves silent. I can see now that, in this investigation, the silences were organised by colour. A few months later another silence came, and everything changed.

*

In Old French, the verb *silencer* means 'to reduce to silence'. This word resonates with my own silence. I imagined that it could have another meaning: to make everything silent, to make yourself silent, to become transparent, and to watch the world turning around you. To create a space, a retreat. My world existed at that precise point, in the dissonance of the space between those two definitions. It is not silence itself which interests me, but its incarnations, its powers – the way it acts in our lives, gaining in strength without our ever being able to grasp it, like a black hole.

*

I often dream of water, of drifting and floods. A few days ago, I saw myself as a child. We were out at sea, on the little family motorboat we used to take out during the summer, while the sun was setting. We used to fish for sardines as we went and grill them the same evening, smelling the strong, acrid smoke. A few hundred metres from the shore, when we had brought the boat to a gentle halt for a few minutes, the sun would dazzle us with its still-burning rays. I would dive into the dark, icy water. Once, all of a sudden, I was terrified, realising that I was alone. Seen from above, my body was a small pale form lost amid an expanse of midnight blue, whose calm surface was slightly ruffled by the wind.

*

When I saw you again for the first time, it was in the kitchen. I was in the same place I am today, looking out of the window. The wind was moving in the top of the big blue-green cypress tree which marks the middle of the long strip of grass rising in a steep slope towards the end of the narrow garden. A strange topography, which reminds us each time we climb towards the big, shabby trees from the edge of the property that we live at the foot of a hill, which people here call a mountain. Further out, the trees become a wood, marking the boundary of the present town, which is a few hundred metres higher, to the east. Then the wood becomes a vast forest, which I had spotted by chance during one of our long walks when the town was in lockdown. Almost without exchanging a word, my partner and I took turns holding our son, who was only a few months old; clasping him to our bodies as though to protect him not only from the cold but from everything that was happening. I returned to the home we shared feeling as though I were filled with a mixture of pure, icy air, winter light and an indescribable warmth. That day, your body was floating just a little to my left, at the level of my temple. It felt as though it was only because you were in my peripheral vision that I could see you, immobile, suspended, as though you were levitating a few centimetres above the ground. I did not dare turn my head to look at you, for fear that you would disappear. I could almost feel the mass of your body; large, heavy, a solid presence, but at the same time, discreet. I thought then, although now I am no longer sure, that you were watching me with a gentle expression, perhaps a little sad. I thought that you had come to watch over me. I concentrated on what was happening on my right. The garden plants had not yet grown very tall, but I could see all their stems, their petals and their leaves vibrating asynchronously, as if they were all connected by an unseen energy which made them resonate – thousands of invisible relationships which made me feel as though I were attending a concert without music. Every plant was performing its own score in its own space for the two of us, their sole silent listeners.

*

I haven't travelled, or barely, for the past two years. This morning, however, I hesitated once more on the doorstep, as though I were out at sea. Distances become so great that they are terrifying. Lines stretch. Memories turn translucent. The light of the screens on which our eyes are fixed every day for hours at a time takes on increasingly cosmic proportions, like the elements of a universe rushing away from each other at exponential speed. As if we were drifting, side by side, in opposite directions. Are we disappearing into ourselves? Or are we slowly going off-course towards an *elsewhere*, all the while thinking we are still connected? Recently I made a rule for myself: never to let a day pass without writing to someone who is, or once was, dear to me. It is a quiet ritual. Every time, it feels as though a point on a map has lit up. An emotional waypoint, like the animated symbols which move slowly before our motionless bodies during noisy long-haul night flights over immense expanses, ink-black and unknown.

*

I was preparing to set out for the first time on what Christian Bili calls 'the trip'. Christian is an artist who works with plants. At that time, he had just begun a project with *Salvia divinorum*, a variety of sage with divinatory powers. According to him, ingesting this plant under certain special conditions opened up spaces not otherwise accessible. His long-term project, which was both scientific and poetic, consisted in allowing various people to travel to these places, so that he could collect accounts of their experiences. Little by little, a map would take shape, bringing together fragmentary images of the invisible continent. The protocol he had given to me specified that once a day for ten days I should mix a teaspoonful of the salvia into a little black tea. In advance of our final brief meeting to discuss the process – which I considered to be serious work – he had processed the leaves into a powder and carefully shaken it into the envelope which I now slipped discreetly into my jacket pocket. He told me: 'The idea is to prepare your body to receive the plant. Since each person has a different level of sensitivity, it's possible that the experience will pass you by completely. And that wouldn't be a huge problem, but in this way certain regions of your brain which are usually inactive will be stimulated. A bit like the salvia was going to start living inside you.' Seeing the surprise, or the unease, in my expression, he added, 'Don't worry. You won't feel anything at all during the day. But it may come to you at night.' I asked him how, and whether I would dream of anything in particular. 'It's very subtle. You'll definitely dream strange dreams, like you've never had before, or the sage will colour your dreams.'

*

In French, the verb 'griser' can mean to blur or grey out, to darken, to excite or to intoxicate. Being in an altered state is thus to be blurred, tinted.

*

Ambient music is discreet. It doesn't 'impose itself on your space … but creates a sort of landscape', according to Brian Eno. He also uses precisely the same term, *tint*, to describe his method: *ambient music* tints the space in which one listens. Just as painters' pigments dissolve into the binder, so music diffuses through the air and colours the silence, colours our listening. By the time *Music for Airports* came out in 1978, Eno had for three years already been constructing music composed of sounds left purposely unfinished, like a sketch, a framework, or an invitation to add the finishing touches to the mix.

*

I see you sitting at the wooden table in the left-hand corner of the living room. Hunched over a pad of graph paper, pencil in hand, you work wordlessly. You count, you plan, you sketch. I watch how meticulously you draw the lines, the precision of your handwriting, of your organisation. From the opposite corner of the room, I try to make sense of your stillness, of the concentration which seems to draw you out of our world. I remember that I tried to match that silence of yours, which could last for several hours at a time. And that I gave it up. I think that everyone who lived in our home at that time did so in an autonomous, silent bubble. Separate but together, just like you and our mother, who were not given to physical affection either. Isolated from each other, our bodies cohabited without contact, in the calm and distant world you had created.

*

According to the musician and critic David Toop, listening is an activity that connects us to the world. It liquefies the boundary between 'what is outside and what is inside'. John Cage described his relationship with music as a redefinition of silence: 'This was Thoreau's notion of music too, you see. Music is continual, he said; it's only listening which is intermittent. I can read to you from the *Journal* long passages written when he was twenty-one years old, if you please, or twenty-two at the most, on the subject of silence. He said silence was like a sphere, and sounds were bubbles on its surface.' Ambient music is like a milieu: it exists between things and their constituent parts. To listen to it invites the question of limits, of the boundary between music and the music of the world, between the human and the non-human, and to become aware – as Toop puts it in a 2019 essay entitled 'How Much World Do You Want?: Ambient Listening and Its Questions' – that this invisible connection can spark a new form of empathy with the world around us. Ambient music maintains an essential relationship with the silence it reveals and inhabits, without ever filling it. It opens up other silences within the silence. It generates multi-dimensional spaces in the sonic cosmos, revealing the matter which is always there linking us with infinite diversity. In a time of 'ubiquitous remote, disembodied connection', the dream of background music which could discreetly accompany our activities and generate multiple daily revelations has, writes Toop, turned on itself. According to an alternative perspective on ambient music, it runs the risk of becoming 'a backdrop to productivity', taking on the role of filling the void in dehumanised workspaces. For Toop, there is only one escape from this misuse: the aesthetic integrity of the music which, according to him, relies on it offering the possibility of withdrawal.

*

In 1975, Judy Nylon, an artist, musician and singer in the New York glam punk and no wave scene, visited her friend Brian Eno, who was bedridden after being hit by a London taxi. She had only a few pounds in her pocket but didn't want to arrive empty-handed. It was raining hard. A man was selling records outside the Tube station. She picked up the first album which looked to her like gentle music, something to help ease her friend's pain. It was an album of Renaissance harp music. 'Neither of us was into harp music,' she told Bart Plantenga, a critic and radio DJ, 'but I grew up in America with ambient music. If I was upset as a kid I was allowed to fall asleep listening to a Martin Denny album… I think it was called *Quiet Village*. The jungle sounds, played very softly, made the room's darkness caressing instead of empty as a void.' Eno was lying down, looking out over the rainy park on Grantully Road. Nylon continues: 'I put the harp music on and balanced it as best as I could from where I stood.' Neither she nor Eno could clearly hear the notes, drowned out as they were by the sound of the rain. '[Eno] caught on immediately to what I was doing and helped me balance the softness of the rain patter with the faint string sound.'

*

In the spring of the first lockdown, I was still working as a lecturer at several art schools. Obliged to teach remotely, I had proposed a research project to the students of one of my seminars which I thought would resonate in an interesting way with the situation in which we all found ourselves. In the archives of Ecart (a Genevan artists' collective co-founded by John M. Armleder, Patrick Lucchini and Claude Rychner in the late 1960s), I found the programme for a concert which Armleder had given in the Hochschule of St. Gallen, Switzerland, in 1981. Entitled 'Mostly Silent Music: A FluxConcert', it included around twenty pieces by composers from John Cage to Terry Riley, taking in Takehisa Kosugi and La Monte Young *en route*. The common thread was that they all centred on silence or quasi-silence, challenging the audience passively, one might say, through the negative, the nothing, the void. This selection of works was an invitation to active listening through strategies to evoke waiting, absence and immobility; strategies built on an economy of means and often verging on the almost-nothing, on a void that would reveal a listening environment at once collective and intimate. During an interview, Armleder told us how he had given this performance, alone on stage. This was not the only context in which 'Mostly Silent Music' was performed; in fact, the programme was just one iteration of a series of variations of a Fluxus concert, solely composed of silent pieces. Armleder performed these works – some musical or poetic, and some largely performance-based or conceptual – one after the other, without hierarchy or emphasis. According to the black-and-white printed programmes we found in the Ecart archives, the pieces had been classified in sequences: 'Piano Pieces' by John Cage, George Brecht and John M. Armleder himself, followed by 'Phonetic Poems' by Christian Morgernstern, Man Ray and Terry Riley; 'Violin Pieces' by Brecht; and, finally, La Monte Young and Robin Page. The concert had ended with a series of 'Other Pieces' by Dick Higgins, Kosugi and Ben Vautier. The final piece, 'Audience' by Vautier, was based on one simple instruction: the performer, in this case Armleder, must stay and do nothing until the last audience member had left the room. In St. Gallen, the artist was confronted with two students who had decided to wait him out. He told us, laughing, that the piece had lasted almost two hours. I could almost feel the density of silence in that near-deserted room during those long, almost motionless minutes of shared presence. The theatre transformed into something like an oversized waiting room.

*

At first, I hadn't paid much attention to this most singular void, the void of the lockdown, perhaps thinking that it was already familiar to me. I would walk the length of the park. The sky was grey but bright over the crowns of the beech trees, above the town which lay arrested in the distance, frozen. The plate-glass windows of the few shops along the street had their metal shutters down and looked as though they had been locked up in haste, as if nobody had bothered to inform their potential customers about a sudden, unplanned closure. But this particular day of inactivity wasn't quite like the rest. Something indefinably different was in the air. Wherever we looked, to left or right, we saw lone, scattered figures walking the road ahead of us, lost in their thoughts. Each of them seemed socially deactivated, advancing without a word, without a glance, in an invisible bubble. Below us, I saw the closed tennis courts. The red clay was ready to be trodden. The nets had been taken down. It seemed that the season was over. In reality, it was just about to start. The marks on the ground, white lines scored through red powder, were like the skeletons of spaces; projections of the buildings in which we were all going to curl up in silence, and for a good while longer.

*

We had been working for several days on what would become our longest building project. We had to repaint the outer walls of a large house that had been left deliberately unoccupied by its owners. Simple and imposing without being luxurious, the house had become dilapidated over time. It was the type of long, repetitive project that you accepted as a meditative act, perhaps to fill the gaps in your order book or perhaps because you knew you'd do a better job than someone else who would have carried it out with no pleasure. When you were commissioned for that kind of work, you made sure it coincided with the school holidays so I could work with you. We had spent the day only metres apart, hardly exchanging a word, with only the distant noise of the town for company and the silent, intermittent caress of the cool air presaging a storm. My mind, almost blank, had become concentrated on the crevices in the surface, on filling them with white – heady, dazzling. It was a little like losing myself in Robert Rauschenberg's white paintings. Back then, though, I wasn't familiar with these works, which Rauschenberg had produced in different variations beginning in the early 1950s. Their immaculate surfaces were the result of applying house paint with a roller, the artist careful to leave no trace of his hand. Some of them were even painted by other people. The white of the *White Paintings* – the simple name Rauschenberg gave them – may invoke a nothingness in the spiritual sense: the absence becoming a horizon, the void an immensity, the nothing an everything. I read somewhere that during this time Rauschenberg didn't always have the money to buy new canvases. Regularly invited to exhibit new paintings, he would reuse those white paintings which hadn't been sold. Obliged to recycle them, he would paint over them in white to make new *White Paintings*. Not only is there no original painting in this series – which is an unusual thing to note for monochrome paintings – but they are also far from being empty. The sedimentation of the multiple layers of paint, as on a wall which has been painted and repainted over and over again, produces an invisible stratification. In these works, the white, I believe, becomes 'full'. It is not silence which emanates from these paintings, but white noise.

*

In the 1970s, the Dutch scientists Hans Kennis and Jos Spijkstra – whose work I discovered in a vintage book on parapsychology – attempted to capture voices from the beyond in the background noise of magnetic tapes. When I became interested in electronic voice phenomena (the presence of the voices of the dead in electronic static), I read that the first person to discover these sounds was Friedrich Jürgenson, a Ukraine-born painter living in Sweden who was also an archaeologist, as well as an opera singer. In the late 1950s, after recording the sounds of the Swedish countryside, he noticed a voice on the tape. He thought at first that he had picked up a radio signal but soon realised that it must be something very different. A man's voice, speaking Norwegian, was describing 'nightly bird voices' amid a jumble of other sounds, fragments and vibrations. The voices which Jürgenson had just discovered were not 'from outer space', as he initially believed, but from beyond the grave. He had invented a technology capable of speaking with the dead. In David Toop's *Ocean of Sound*, I found a reference to Konstantīn Raudive, a Latvian writer and researcher who had been a student of Carl G. Jung and who continued Jürgenson's work, beginning in the mid-1960s. Toop recalls Raudive's belief that by leaving a tape recorder switched on in a silent room, he could capture the voices of the deceased. Toop then asks himself: these 'psychophonic' voices, heard in the 'so-called silence' of our modern cities, are 'spirits trying to tell us something. But what?' Some years after hearing the male voice speaking Norwegian, Friedrich Jürgenson heard his own dead mother talking to him on one of his recordings. That day, Jürgenson abandoned painting to dedicate himself entirely to his 'audioscopic research'.

*

Rauschenberg compared the *White Paintings* to clocks, their immaculate surfaces taking on new appearances with the trajectory of the sun. In the calm of an autumn afternoon in the Stable Gallery in New York, where they were exhibited in 1961, I imagine them taking on the shadow of a cloud passing outside the window, or the intensity of daylight, depending on the season. The passage of time would be reflected on the white paintings, watches without hands, silent presences animated by the cosmic movements of weather and stars.

*

I was surprised by the void in certain Swiss cities which are almost entirely deserted at the weekend, once the offices have emptied, and which are only, mechanically, refilled again first thing on Monday morning. Between times, I remember wandering as if in a waking dream through those depopulated landscapes, encountering only a few isolated figures who had stayed to work after hours, or for maintenance of these deserted places – tower blocks, factories, studios, office spaces, bars, shops and restaurants with closed shutters – built for those who had gone away. The others, I thought to myself (since there were surely people who lived there) must all be hiding. I would imagine even those people trying, perhaps, to convince themselves that this empty theatre, suddenly deserted, was not entirely unreal.

*

You stayed a little later that evening. I see you with your back to me on the scaffolding, concentrating, wordlessly applying the paint roller to the worn plaster, leaving a thick layer of fresh colour. Doing things together, like working, was a pleasant way to experience the silence which existed between us. Perhaps it gave us an excuse not to talk to each other. We had to concentrate so as not to make mistakes. The background noise of the radio which accompanied you to every job site provided a kind of framework for reflection to the lack of words. The songs were always the same but played in a slightly different order, so that they stood out from the general soundscape. Occasionally, they were jumping-off points for my daydreams. That is my version of elevator music. My ambient. I think that I learned to love that with you: looking at a wall, a sheet of wallpaper, a garden, and listening without speaking, at a distance, to sentimental music, far away, on the radio. It was as though I were entering the space, the silence and the sounds themselves, no longer hearing the melodies or the words. The textures stretch, the rhythms liquefy. Something of those perceived waves remains in my cells, as though this scaffolding music were still filtering through me.

*

It didn't take long for me and the three artists who were taking part in the research on 'Mostly Silent Music' – Elia Fidanza, Léonard Gremaud and Laura Laigo – to come up with the idea for a new collective performance, like a silent ritual, based on Armleder's programme. It seemed to us to echo our situation: isolated, scattered, with no chance of making the thing public. We opened dossiers and filled them with documentation for each piece in Armleder's inaugural programme: scores or instructions, photographs, recordings, videos, films, texts… For certain pieces, the materials at our disposal were incomplete and the artist's memories were not precise enough to tell us exactly which piece was referred to. These empty spaces called for a form of interpretation. Though some specific scores were missing, one work in particular had never left Armleder's mind. To his lasting regret, he told us, he had never – for obvious safety reasons – been able to perform La Monte Young's *Composition 1960 #2*, whose instructions begin with 'Build a fire in front of the audience.' Then it describes how the fire determines the duration of the piece. The performer is invited simply to sit near the fire, watching it burn and, if they have a microphone, to place it close to the flames to amplify their continuous, hypnotic crackle.

*

The void of a bright winter morning in Stockholm. I had arrived at the art school a little ahead of schedule to finish preparing for a conference. The corridors were clean and untouched. Surprised by the silence, I thought that the school must still be closed and anxiously searched for a fellow human to confirm that I hadn't come on the wrong day. But at a half-open door I discovered with astonishment that in reality the students were all already at work, cloistered in their studios, in almost perfect silence.

*

I look at your large, beautiful hands; worn hands with clean-cut nails, searching for a cigarette in a supple packet. The flecks of brown tobacco. The spots of paint on worn-out clothes, paint matting your hair. The smell of beer in the warmth of the evening. Your watery gaze, as though your body were flooding; an overflow of emotion after the second pint. It was in this exact place, sitting at the steel counter, that you told me your sorrow. The first and only time you put words to your distance, to your silence. You spoke about the lack of touch and love, about coldness. You didn't use those words.

It lasted only seconds. And then I saw your eyes shining as you bantered with the young, smiling waitress. I still hear your voice giving me careful instructions, telling me tomorrow's schedule – which I would always forget immediately. Men and women were cheerfully calling out to each other across the bar. The flickering light of the neon signs, ice-cold air conditioning, fatigue. Behind this wall, outside, in the vast car park, the heat was stifling. I couldn't answer. I closed my eyes in the golden light. Open windows on the drive home. No one had been warned that we would be back late. On either side of the road ran a disorderly patchwork of tarmac and plant life. I loved it; I made myself at one, through all the pores of my skin, with these generic landscapes, the business parks and suburban sprawl. We weren't content just to live there. I think we hid there together. It was in that bar a little way back from the supermarket, far from everywhere, that you liked to go and sit, alone, sometimes with me, at the end of the day, and gaze off into the void. You always tried to prolong that moment, I understand now, a little longer each time. You liked to go on walks in deserted places; you liked to search for out-of-the-way spaces on the outskirts of towns. It seems obvious: you were avoiding the centres, the crowds. Were you hiding? Or were you trying to protect yourself, to fade away? I've done the same thing myself, like a private prayer: wandering at random, losing myself in industrial parks which all resemble each other, which are all reassuring. I have watched the nothingness through your eyes, as they became blanker and blanker, and made it part of myself. I have loved detours, peripheries, loved making them the centre, but I have always returned. It's strange to think that 'fade away' can mean both to no longer be visible and to die. You did both. You made yourself absent for a certain time. Little by little, you left the backdrop of our lives. Then you stopped breathing. Your pulse stopped beating. I wasn't there. And in a way, neither were you.

*

What struck us, Elia, Léonard, Laura and me, was that not a single woman featured in the 1981 programme for 'Mostly Silent Music'. We rapidly decided that our project would not be a reconstitution of Armleder's soirée but a complete reconstruction, including rewriting the programme to incorporate instructions by other artists. And so, pieces by Yoko Ono, Alison Knowles and Joan Jonas joined the list. One of the trails Elia Fidanza was following brought us to the idea of water and fluidity, of flow and silence. Notably, we looked into how we might recreate a series by Mieko Shiomi entitled *Water Music*, in which the artist collects different volumes of water in various receptacles, then tips them out. The instructions relied on the phrase 'LET THE WATER LOSE ITS STILL FORM' – or, in other words, 'let the water flow/lose its tranquil (fixed, static, immobile, even silent) form,' since 'still' can also mean 'silent'. Silent flow is also the theme of another series, inspired by the inaugural programme of 'Mostly Silent Music': George Brecht's *Drip Music* (1959–1962). These 'events' consisted in pouring liquid from one receptacle, such as a watering can or an earthenware vase, into another – perhaps a plate, or a tray. The duration of the performance is the time taken decanting. While researching Brecht, I realised that Eno had cited *Drip Music* as one of his foundational sources of inspiration. He had even performed it while he was still a student at the Winchester School of Art in the late 1960s. We could say that for him, it represented a gateway into a new conception of music: spatial, experimental, based on duration, attention and listening. We had something. A constellation was forming, linking Shiomi's silent flow, Brecht's poetic 'waterfalls' and the raindrops which transformed themselves into music for Eno. As we were planning the staging of the performance, international travel was banned once again and our programme was cancelled, stayed at the project stage, existed only on paper.

*

The burning void which I loved so much when, at the heart of summer, mind numbed by long floating weeks drifting aimlessly without schedule, in a few moments of meditation there came the culmination, euphoric, like a drug suddenly released into the atmosphere – an absence from the rest of the world, carrying within it every possibility. I preserve this heat in the hollow of my body like a treasure, as if time were suddenly opening up, freeing itself; as if for the space of a moment, it secretly belonged to me.

*

In 'Towards a Feminism of the Void', the English philosopher Nina Power asks us to consider the possibility that 'the void ... [is] perhaps "the" object "of" feminism'. A paradoxical hypothesis, because in response to the objectification of the body, its instrumentalisation, its dispossession, there arises, according to Power, another perspective which lends to this nothing the status of something, leading to a double domination, a double appropriation: firstly the appropriation of the female body which makes it into a *thing*, one which unlike the male body is thought to be *lacking* 'reason, a cock, strength', and secondly the appropriation of the void itself, of the silence to which the female body has been subjected, allowing men – whether artists, writers or philosophers – to produce works, books and theories on the subject of the double void which they themselves created. At the very beginning of this 2017 essay, Power reproduces a text by the Californian artist Audrey Wollen: 'BEWARE MALE ARTISTS MAKING ARTWORK ABOUT EMPTINESS / NOTHING DOES NOT BELONG TO YOU / GIRLS OWN THE VOID / BACK OFF *FUCKERS*!!!!' Accompanying this text is a group of archival images arranged by Wollen which shows men's work around the void, from *Le Vide* (The Void) by Yves Klein to Robert Barry's *Inert Gas Series* and the almost empty sheet music for John Cage's *4'33"*. Wollen's work is based notably on what she calls 'Sad Girl Theory', which explores female sadness as a form of resistance. Power proposes that we take Wollen's void seriously, using it as a foundation for a 'declaration of resistance' to men talking about and creating work on nothingness – a boycott of the 'agents of the visible, colonisers of the void'. Power believes that the void must be liberated from male domination and resituated in another history which has manifestly been 'voided': the story of these voids and the other, invisible, voids.

*

In 1968, Vija Celmins began drawing oceans. In a multitude of hues on the spectrum from black to white, taking in every shade of grey, these works reproduce close-up views of the wave-ruffled surface of the sea. This series, which is still in progress, unfolds in minuscule variations with constant similarities and differences, centred on a single idea, on the same image. I imagine this series to be infinite.

*

A few months ago, I met Anna Raimondo. As a politically engaged nomad artist, she has often used sound, the body and the voice as artistic mediums. I wanted to ask her about the political dimension of the radio pieces which she often deploys in public spaces. We were sitting in her studio in Brussels. The director Guillaume Abgrall was recording sound all over the building. Raimondo proposed that we all get closer together. We sat in front of her computer and she played us *Derrière la mer* (Behind the Sea), one of her recent sound installations. Based on interviews that she has conducted in various countries, the piece features individuals describing their relationship with the sea, one by one. I don't know why, but I remember that at some point we all lowered our eyes as though to hear better. The interview responses are beautiful, powerful, vulnerable. The sea is sometimes a matrix of pleasure, sometimes threatening, sometimes immense and mysterious, sometimes fragile and on the point of disappearing. The words seem at times to melt into the sound, to become pure vibration or mystical chant. In the middle of our conversation, silence fell for a moment and I had the feeling that the phrases were still being spoken, only in our heads. Raimondo told me later: 'The problem isn't in giving people who are unheard the chance to speak, but in learning to listen.'

*

We were in the bedroom, the only place in this house (a kind of massive urban chalet built entirely of wood) where we could have the space and the privacy we needed for the trip. We had been preparing for several weeks. We had drawn the curtains to dim the light. Christian was rolling the leaves in his hand, a little like rolling a cigar. Meanwhile, I was brushing my teeth in the en-suite so that, as he had explained, the slight irritation of the brush on my gums would stimulate the parts of my mouth which would come into contact with the salvia. He explained that the oldest and driest leaves had to be in the middle of the roll, which I would soon be chewing on for an extended period, and that the youngest and supplest would be on the outside. I remember that once I was stretched out on several blankets which had been laid on the carpet near the bed, I saw his hand holding a phone screen in front of me. He asked me to concentrate on it, just in case. 'We are here and now. If you get lost, I want you to remember the information here so that you can find your way back again.'

*

In *The Mother of All Questions*, Rebecca Solnit writes that there is a difference between silence and quiet: '*silence* as what is imposed and *quiet* as what is sought.'

*

You often described us as 'the little people'. I didn't understand. I saw us as big, important. I thought we were free. With hindsight, it's true that I almost never came across you in the middle of a casual conversation with strangers. I only remember the anger you sometimes expressed towards certain people, perhaps people who were richer than us, or who you reckoned were snobs. But I don't have any memories of just listening to you speak.

*

The moment in scenes of violence and trauma in certain films when the sound is suddenly cut. The deaf-mute vision of a world whose intensity becomes purely visual, as though emotion had saturated the spectrum of sound, imposing its noise on the noise, rendering it imperceptible, cancelling it out.

*

The ocean drawings were developed alongside views of desert sand, of starry skies. These works are based on modes of observation that are almost choreographic: look at the sea, bend down towards the ground, raise your eyes to the night sky. Simple movements which form part of a process of elimination. Vija Celmins is attempting, piece by piece, element by element, to remove everything she judges inessential, to the greatest possible extent, leaving only what makes a piece of art. Her works are often discussed as references to immensity, to the void, to the cosmos. For my part, I see in them a need for connection as much as an evocation of distance. I see in them the opposite of nothingness, something like an emotional density born of listening. 'The paintings tend to have an internal feeling, as if there was something behind what you see.' As the artist draws or paints from photographs, reproducing them, I imagine her entering the depths of the image. I imagine her as if in a melding of senses, listening to these oceans, eyes fixed on the horizon. Water fills the image like the emotions that submerge us.

*

I found out recently that you had been back in contact with your father. A nameless man you never mentioned in front of me. I only knew – and that only because I had insisted on being told – that he had left and never come back. One day you got a call from someone who told you that your father was somewhere, so alone and so poor that he could no longer look after himself, and that you had to help him. He was living in a caravan. You were the only person left who could support him. I don't know if you had ever tried to find out whether your father was still alive. You didn't say anything. You didn't go to meet this man with whom you had had no contact since you were a child. I don't know much about him. A little photograph found at the bottom of a box, where he stands straight and austere in a big, dark overcoat, next to your mother and you as a child. Muddled information about a childhood darkened by his presence, his departure which came perhaps as a relief, and that he might have come from a family of shepherds from central France. I would have liked to talk to you about those unsaid things. About this silence between you, between us. About what it was that made you not want to talk to him for more than thirty years. About your silence when the telephone rang. That time, I was there. My sister and I were watching you from the other side of the room. You turned your back on us. It must have been about 8pm. We were having dinner. Nothing had prepared us for this news except maybe the fact that our mother had gone away without us, which had never happened before. Someone on the other end of the line said two or three sentences to you. You made a strange sound which frightened us. A violent noise: a shout, a choked sound. You began to cry. Georges, our other grandfather, the one we knew, had just died. I would never have guessed that you had secretly, with almost no outward sign, adopted this man as your own father. Your back was racked with spasms. It was as if a huge block of emotions was forcing its way out of your body. A few seconds later you rejoined us. Your body had turned back into the compact and stable mass I had always known. The tragedy had not, in appearance, lasted more than a few seconds, but the fracture had let a strange light escape.

*

Every one of Celmins' pieces has so much detail that it takes on an almost mineral density. In fact, each one is loaded with such a burden of time, of concentration, of hand movements and graphite marks on the white surface of the paper that it becomes an exhibition of matter. We are looking not at an image of the ocean, but at a concrete presence: an expanse of carbon. Laid out according to a certain order, the image is formed from the meeting between this fragment of mineral, this dust and its vibration on the rough white surface of the paper. Graphite and diamond are composed of the same chemical element, carbon, but their structures are different: one is denser, and lets the light through. And yet, for Celmins, reproducing the image of a starry sky is first and foremost an exploration of the colour black, the colour of her materials – the material of the night.

*

I turned my back on that life and on the town where we lived. I rejected what suddenly appeared to me as injustice: that your body was progressively being broken down, that dust was filling your lungs, that your skin cracked under the cement that desiccated it; and I didn't want that for myself either. I didn't want my back to give out, my nose to bleed, my feet to suffer like yours did. I wanted to save you, but I was the one who left. I had the thought, once: *obviously.* It was at the end of a long day on a particularly difficult building site that I felt that impulse for the first time. It was as though I had thrown myself into the void. I got onto my bike without bothering to change my clothes. You were still working. I put my foot on the pedal and pushed off, riding as fast as I could. My anger rose along with my speed. Until everything was clear. A clarity I had never experienced before. Rage and lucidity. I would never have thought that they could go together so well. That evening, I made a pact with the rain, the asphalt and the light. Launched at top speed towards the bright horizon, I began to scream at the top of my lungs. The rain lashed my face, as if all the water in the world had come to sweep away my drowned body.

*

For years and years, I didn't know how to talk. Not *really* talk. When I finally let the words out, it felt as though I spent nearly a year crying almost constantly.

*

I see myself on a spring evening sitting on the edge of the beach, its reliefs made so jagged by erosion that it reminded me of lace, a geological lacework of sand and sharp-edged rocks and, at least in my memory, sun-bleached ruins among which I had walked earlier that afternoon. I was scrutinising the black waves, which were breaking noisily onto the shore and rolling over themselves. I suddenly felt invaded, as though my heart were exploding in my chest in time with the pounding movement of the water. A few hundred metres to my right, lost in the darkness, the brittle rocks beneath my feet were, like me, confronting the invisible horizon. I was shaken by a sob, and it felt like the water of the Mediterranean was entering my body and catching me up in a wave of sadness so foreign and intense that it nauseated me.

*

Certain works of art, certain sonorities – like those of the sea – are mirrors. The emotions they provoke are not pre-defined but rather reflect whatever the observer is feeling. If you are happy, they make you feel like everything is fine. If you are sad, they transform themselves into lamentations. As Celmins put it in one of her notebooks: 'the first look at a wave should (maybe) (if only for a moment) be reminiscent of being in love – a feeling of Oh – of surprise, of senses waking up.'

*

The last thing I could remember seeing before I closed my eyes was Christian. He was thanking the higher powers responsible for the trip I was about to take. Turning his body 90 degrees with each incantation, he had addressed the four points of the compass. The almost unbearable bitterness of the leaves filled my mouth with saliva which I was absolutely forbidden to spit out. When I opened my eyes a crack he was still there, much closer than I had imagined, sitting on the sofa, stoic, looking towards the window, solemnly keeping vigil over my trip.

*

'The image [in my drawings],' says Celmins, 'is just a sort of armature.' A structure, a skeleton around which she constructs a space, a form. The image of an ocean is, as she explains in an interview with the artist Chuck Close, 'almost nothing'. Paradoxically, it is the search for this void which gives her pieces their materiality, almost entirely freed as they are from the duty of representation – their physical presence. Celmins does not copy her photographic sources, she reproduces them like a performance. She has made it a rule to work without regret. If there is a mistake in an image, that image is immediately discarded. Around the series of ocean drawings which is visible today, I realise, there is ranged a constellation of works that are invisible, deleted, erased. The images between the images, like the silences between notes.

*

Night, not far from Paris. A concert. Near-darkness. Pure improvisation. Solid. The trip was long, sinuous, punctuated by explosions and epiphanies, by moments of absolute sweetness. Feeling yourself falling into a hole, into time. Fleeting impressions, breaths. Being almost paralysed by concentration. Exhalations, static. Hearing these signals as though through a sonic magnifying glass, at the limits of perception.

Towards the end of the concert one of the musicians, at the centre of the stage, ceased playing. Impossible to tell whether the concert was over. No applause. A fraction of a second later, the music started again. After a few moments, it ceased once more for a time that seemed infinite. Then it started again, as though to construct something around this silence, this invisible fire we were beginning to share. Finally, the saxophonist lowered his gaze and let his shoulders relax in an exhalation. I remember the extraordinary quality of this final silence. It illuminated all the preceding silences and revealed that nobody, neither the musicians nor the audience, knew whether the concert would continue. The depth of this silence put us all on hold. For a fraction of a second, our listening attention played the role of a tight-rope walker on an invisible cord. What happened in this suspended instant was a kind of balancing act in which each one of us was simultaneously spectator and performer. That night, I saw a circle of silence forming, and all of us, whether on the stage or in the auditorium, were gathered within it, connected. When the music stopped, it was as if we had been washed up on shore, the water on which we had travelled having receded. I knew then that I was back, but I couldn't tell exactly where. It wasn't important. What I understood then, what the silence revealed to me, was that we had all been sailing, navigating, without a map.

*

When we shared photographs, I brought one that shows you in the middle, to my mother's right, with my sister and me on either side. Lit from the front, we stand out against the dark background. It is night-time and we are wearing evening dress. It must have been taken at a wedding or a family gathering. Our mother is wearing a dress, which is unusual enough to be notable. She is smiling. The dress is sky-blue lace in a light material. That tells me that it was spring or summer. My sister must be six or seven years old. She looks like a little princess, but a slightly wild one. She looks happy. As for me, I look rather shy. More than thirty years later, I still don't like having my photo taken. In the picture, I mainly seem proud to be wearing a suit jacket and posing next to my parents. You, meanwhile, are wearing beige chinos which I don't remember. Your new shoes seem to have been bought for the occasion. You have a smart dark jacket on, but it's a little large in the shoulders. You're wearing the white shirt that you used to put on for every evening occasion. One of the essential elements of your evening dress, although you can't see it in the photo, was the scent you used to wear every time we went out, which you would put on before we left the house and which diffused through every room while you were getting ready. You would put on your city clothes, the clothes that weren't for work and weren't spattered with cement or paint; the clothes that meant we were dressed up and ready to shine. Examining the photo, I notice something strange: while our mother is holding my sister by the hand, you are standing slightly behind the rest of us, as though in a separate sphere. Your arms are hanging by your sides, as if you were floating. Your face is relaxed, but you're the only one of us four who isn't smiling. But you don't look sad, either. You seem to be standing in silence while the party around you is teeming, chaotic, noisy, like Watteau's early 18th-century Pierrot. I don't know why, but this painting has fascinated me since I first saw it as a student at the École du Louvre. At the centre of the image is a person dressed all in white, in what is perhaps a theatre costume, who seems to be levitating. He is in exactly the same pose as you are in the photograph. Behind him, on a lower plane, under something resembling an invisible, imaginary stage, various enigmatic characters busy themselves, smiling. *He* doesn't hear them. Is he in another reality? Is he alone in his own world? Does he represent a ghost? Today, this painting has a title. When it was painted, it had none. In fact, none of Watteau's paintings have titles. Watteau is, they say, an artist of silence. In Pierre Michon's 1990 text *Je veux me divertir* (I Want to Entertain Myself), which the writer dedicated to this enigma which has been haunting me now for a long time, we learn that Watteau was very ill when he painted his Pierrot. In Michon's account, we find a scene describing how the artist introduced himself to the man who would play Pierrot in his painting. Michon writes that Watteau appears to his model, who was the curate of a small town in eastern France, like 'a spectre at daybreak'. You, in the photograph, are a spectre at sunset. At that time in our lives you must already have been drawing back, but we hadn't noticed. It is as if the image reveals not your presence but your absence, your ghostliness. Almost as if, even though you were with us, on the inside you were turning your back on us; as though you were looking elsewhere, towards the shadows, leaving us behind you.

*

When Charles Ray made *Ink Box* in 1986, he had just finished a series of performances in a warehouse he was renting on Venice Beach. It was then that he realised that he wasn't comfortable including his own body in his work. And yet the body, its figuration and the question of presence had always been essential in his approach to sculpture. He was obsessed by the enigmatic expression worn by an ancient Egyptian sculpture in the Metropolitan Museum of New York, a young man stepping forwards with his arms at his sides. Ray described it as 'a meaning machine'. This work, which dates back to the 6th century BCE, is one of the very first life-sized sculptures. In *Ink Box*, the body is replaced by a liquid, its representation by a 91cm^3 cube. Filled with black ink, the geometric form presents an open face on the top, but it is impossible to tell at first whether the surface is solid or liquid. I remember the historian Jean-Pierre Criqui's text on Tony Smith's 1962 sculpture *Die*, which is also dark and cubic. Criqui suggests notably that Smith's piece, which plays on the double sense of its name, relates to the presence of an absent body and is reminiscent of the kouroi of Ancient Greece, placed on tombs as a substitute form for the dead.

*

In the first few months after my arrival in Berlin, black spots began to appear in my vision. At the time, my life was split between several different cities. This lifestyle, which had me travelling by plane four times a week, now seems inconceivable. I immediately consulted a neurologist friend, who said, 'Most of the time it's really nothing serious. You must just be tired.' I was indeed often in an indeterminate state between dream and waking. A slightly unstable state, but one of permanent motion, a little like the stationary flight of certain insects and birds. After looking into it, I discovered that these black dots are called *mouches volantes* (flying flies) in French. In English, they are 'floaters'.

*

'The silence of the sea is mere appearance,' writes Michel Serres in *Genèse* (Genesis). According to the philosopher, it is in this 'sea noise' that we find 'the origin'. But the origin of what? The origin of noise, of background noise, cousin of malaise and rage? '*Noise* and nausea, *noise* and the nautical, *noise* and navy all belong to the same family.' 'We never hear what we call "background noise" as well as we do by the sea.' 'This word *noise* crosses the seas … In Old French, it used to mean: noise, uproar and wrangling; English borrowed the sound from us; we keep only the fury.' *La noise* (quarrel) and *le bruit* (noise) return, for 'our language [has since been] cleansed of this "noise".'

*

When we saw each other again after long years of silence, you were living in a small and extraordinarily tidy flat. But it wasn't the tidiness that really struck me. I knew that you liked things that way, at least since your years in the navy and then the air force. Incidentally, when I think of you, a certain black-and-white photograph often comes to mind. It used to be displayed in our house, along with several other souvenirs of far-flung places which I found mysterious: a taxidermised giant tortoise, a machete for slashing your way through the bush and a black compass, solidly built but worn. In the picture you are young, very thin, and your hair is still almost blond. It would darken later, probably around the time you left the air force. Speaking of the air force, you're wearing aviator shades and a white t-shirt which give you an American look. You're handsome. You're half-smiling. You seem free. But no, what really struck me was that your flat was almost empty. There was a near-clinical cleanliness about everything, or almost everything. When you opened a cupboard to offer me something to drink, I saw identical jars of jam lined up, all their labels facing in the same direction. I only vaguely remember what we talked about: my projects, your walks in the forest? I can no longer remember which detail it was that sent me years back into the past, to long before you left; the coffee was dripping into the pot, filtered through a sheet of kitchen towel because you thought that coffee filters were an unnecessary expense. This was your flat, but it looked like you were camping in it. It looked like a place under siege, everything rationalised and rationed. I felt that you might leave at any moment. Perhaps a go bag was already waiting in a corner. I glanced towards your bed, which was, naturally, impeccably made. In pride of place above it was a large, framed picture which showed a bird taking flight above a body of water, or the sea. A swan or, perhaps, a phoenix, caught in a whirl of blues.

*

Lying supine on several blankets, I waited wordlessly for the salvia to take effect. I didn't want to go to sleep, and I didn't want to get up and leave. I hadn't made it through the first part of the trip just to give up now. I remained perfectly still, eyes closed, gently swallowing down the bitter juice of the leaves; impatient but calm, as though levitating slightly inside myself. Only milliseconds after deciding that the experiment wasn't going to work, I forgot those long minutes of waiting. In the chronology of visions which succeeded one another behind my eyelids, the first was that of a vast starry sky transforming itself into immense domes.

*

Yesterday evening I was sitting out in the garden. Taking advantage of a moment of calm, I had reimmersed myself in a poetry collection which I had bought several weeks earlier. Up to that point, I hadn't been able to get past the first few pages. Our son was asleep upstairs. We had left all the windows open so that we would be able to hear him if he woke up. When night had almost entirely fallen, I noticed that the sun had disappeared. Half-reclining with my head tilted back, I scrutinised all the bright dots studding the clear night sky. I wondered which one was yours. Some people say that when we die, we become celestial bodies. Bright. A body that shines. For a long time, I thought of death only as a form of extinction, of extinguishing. Neither you nor my mother were religious or spiritual. Your views on life and death were profoundly materialistic, in the original sense of the word. I used to imagine the end like a candle being snuffed out. The dying breath, the fading light, then nothing, just flesh, fluids and hair which would nourish the earth, which would bring forth another life, which would generate another, and so on and so forth. I had never imagined that death could be the exact opposite of that image. Perhaps when we are dying, our bodies fill with light and that is how we know that the end is near, that we are about to leave this reality. As for you, when they called to tell us that you had to leave your little flat in the town centre and go to live in a facility with other people who couldn't look after themselves, it was because you had just been discovered one night by the police. They told us that you had been opening the graves in the cemetery a few hundred metres from your home, past the military barracks which face the big square where, when I was a child, they held all the noisy celebrations that came back around almost identically every year: carnival, funfair, concert, circus. You were lifting the thick, heavy stones that sealed the tombs. I imagine that you were looking for ghosts, or that you wanted to set them free so you could speak to them. Perhaps you wanted to pass over to the other side yourself, to go into the night. One day you told me something about death. You said that when you were young (much younger than I am today), you had accepted the fact that your life had less value than the lives of those who were dependent on you. I would always remember the way you spoke about death, about the death that walked beside you, which was there within you, as if that day you had destroyed some part of yourself, reduced it to silence. You saw ghosts, too. You already had something, nevertheless, that shone from the inside. There are so many stars, so many silent presences, so much distance. In the collection I was reading before I dozed off and forgot all about the sunset, the author was describing a vanished world, somewhere around what is now Nebraska in the United States, where the Skidi band of the Pawnee Nation lived. Each village, each individual, had their own star in the firmament. I had also read in another book about one of the last inhabitants of the Hopi villages that if there was a problem, if someone fell ill, that person would be reconnected to their celestial body by the intervention of a Star Priest whose entire body was painted with stars, forming a constellation. I understood that for this civilisation, illness was the consequence of a cosmic disconnection. While you were excavating graves, I was searching the celestial vault, trying to find your star. I was thinking of the vestiges of those lost worlds, and you – you were shining in the sky overhead.

*

Coming through the door, I stepped into a bright, colourful world, so clear and shining that it looked like a drawing. I had touched down in the universe of my childhood, which I saw as if through a transparent film which allowed me to observe, in silence and in great detail, all the people coming and going. But I was still separated from the world by this membrane which, for some unknown reason, seemed to be vacuum sealed. It took on the forms of my surroundings, which looked close enough to touch but from which I was completely cut off. I was in two places at once, as if cloned. My first body was lying in the bedroom of the big wooden house, on a silent weekday, just outside town. My second was under a transparent, raised floor which allowed me to observe the emotional ecosystem of my first years of conscious life. My sister was playing, concentrated on her toy figures, on a large tree trunk in front of our home. I had completely forgotten the existence of that felled tree. We had spent so many hours silently observing the rings in the wood, the lines of time, the imagined growth of that immense being. I saw my father getting out of his van, but I couldn't hear any sound. I remembered that white van, its rattling engine. He didn't see me; with his aviator shades on, he was walking with purpose towards my mother, who was sitting on the concrete steps of the block of flats where we lived back then. A cigarette in her hand, a blank expression on her face.

*

The grey sea comes alive, the swell reveals itself to be 'a coloured wall' of noises, of every noise, as Michel Serres writes. 'This restlessness is within hearing, just shy of definite signals, just shy of silence … Background noise may well be the ground of our being,' he continues. 'The background noise never ceases; it is limitless, it is continuous, unending, unchanging … How much noise must be made to silence noise? And what terrible fury puts fury in order? … Every call, every signal, must be separated from the hubbub that occupies silence, in order to be, to be perceived … Yes,' he writes, 'noise is metaphysical … One hears its subliminal huffing and soughing on the high seas.' '*Noise* … is original hatred. We hear it on the high seas.' 'We have to recognise her in the midst of the coloured wall of the swell.' 'It is the ensemble of possible profiles, the sum of horizons.'

*

Last winter, I interviewed the writer and essayist Pacôme Thiellement about a musical project he had collaborated on with the composer Delphine Dora. *confinés depuis la nuit des temps* (locked down since the dawn of time) is a musical sound field which sets an improvisation by Thiellement to music. He sent his piece to Dora over the phone, as voicemails. She used them to create a musical montage haunted by Thiellement's voice, combining her own compositions with fragments of other pieces including works by Else-Marie Pade, Kali Malone and John Tilbury, to form a soundscape that is sombre, solemn, intensely cinematographic. The result is a dense plunge into the darkness of that period in our lives, lit by the flashes of Thiellement's thoughts. We spoke online, each of us in their own home, in different cities. 'The lockdown we're experiencing now is a repetition of our original confinement,' Thiellement explained. I squinted at my screen; he was backlit. I could only see a dark silhouette; his long hair and beard made him look like an oracle. 'Why is it that when something like this happens, we do nothing but experience it from the inside?' His voice booms out at the beginning of the piece. 'We never escape it in our lives, only postpone it,' Thiellement continues. 'We're going to have to face it, and lockdown is the right time to face it.'

*

I left for a decade or so. The few memories I have of you during that interval are like a dotted line in the chronology of our relationship. Your distant voice, unfamiliar and vulnerable over the phone. The words you had to search for. A meal which went on too long. Several years later, I managed to come back. I drove with a friend. I remember it very well. The weather was very clear, very cold. We drove in silence, my chest tight. After turning in through the outer wall of the verdant, slightly out-of-the-way property, we parked. I hesitated for a moment, hands on the steering wheel, staring through the windscreen at a field of maize swaying in the wind. She said she would wait for me. As I walked away, almost paralysed by emotion, I felt her gaze following me towards the entrance of the building from the passenger seat. The door was opened for me. I turned towards it and you appeared. You were standing immobile in the sun-bathed entrance hall. I saw deep in your eyes that you recognised me. For a moment I caught sight of that light in your faded blue eyes which said everything. You could no longer speak, but you knew who I was. You took me by the hand. The carer said that you liked to go and see the green space outside. We walked in the freezing wind until I noticed that you weren't dressed for the weather and that you were cold. After that, without a word, you showed me everything that filled your days. Your room; the gym clothes my sister had brought for you, clean and carefully folded. Your treasure, the sweets you stole in a spirit of mischief from the other residents, hidden away in a secret box. The communal television which you invited me to watch with you. All the same, I realised very quickly that it was difficult for you to concentrate. I pretended not to notice the other people there, who were agitated and noisy. We stayed like that, looking at the screen without really seeing it, until the emotions submerged me. On the way home, turning my back on you for the last time, tears flooding my eyes, all at once the town around me was blurred and peaceful.

*

Ink Box, Charles Ray's sculpture, could be considered a liquid ghost. Approximately one cubic metre of darkness, the presence of an absent body, its unsettling and elusive materiality. This piece poses similar questions to those raised by Robert Rauschenberg's *White Paintings* and, unexpectedly, represents in a certain sense their negative. Responding to the immaculate white of the canvas is the cube of ink, like the potentiality of something waiting to be written, formed or printed. The white paintings are surfaces, invisible images; projection screens for a possibility. This cube of black ink and these white paintings made with paint rollers are the two faces of what the philosopher Giorgio Agamben calls 'pure potentiality'. Near the end of *Potentialities*, in the sub-chapter entitled 'Matter', he explores the possibilities of 'this writing of the potentiality that no one writes'. This is connected to the idea of a writing which 'is not a form' but which 'experiences itself', like 'a writing tablet that suffers not the impression of a form'. According to Agamben, 'the trace is nothing other than the most rigorous attempt to reconsider – against the primacy of actuality and form – the Aristotelian paradox of potentiality, the gesture of the scribe who dips his pen in thought and writes solely with his potentiality (not to write).'

*

I came back to the bedroom. Christian was still sitting in the same place, keeping me in the corner of his eye so he could make sure I was all right. It took me a while to regain consciousness. For several minutes, I was bobbing just under the surface. I felt my body floating in the room, then setting itself down astonishingly gently, like a leaf falling from a tree, or as if I had become the leaf of the salvia I had just absorbed. After a few moments, Christian invited me to sit with him and asked me to describe where I had been, to draw what I had seen. Strangely, all I could remember was the immense, deep, bright night and the alignment of a group of celestial bodies which were moving and forming a bright rose window in motion, like a cosmic door, an invitation. I still remember how the beginning of the experiment felt; I remember my body falling in reverse, from the ground to the sky, from the Earth to the stars, approaching that stellar opening, plunging towards the unknown. I also have the feeling that I wasn't alone in that trip, which was in a vehicle, a train or a bus, but I don't know who was with me.

*

'We are confined to the Earth,' Thiellement explains. Human beings have been trying to leave for a long time, but we haven't yet succeeded. 'We are confined to the universe. We are confined to our bodies. But the ultimate confinement is death.' The final confinement is symbolised by the grave, the stone, the coffin which is sealed and buried. Thiellement's text also reminds us that certain avant-garde writers, from Emily Dickinson to René Daumal – he quotes Daumal's novel *La Grande Beuverie* (A Night of Serious Drinking) – have tried to discover themselves through solitude and deprivation, detachment and reclusion. 'You have just one thing in common, loneliness.' For the writer this solitude, this confinement, whether it is innate or current, is what we all share. Thiellement uses the metaphor of a party: 'I've never been to many parties. Although I loved seeing people. But when I found myself at a party I always felt uneasy; I felt even more alone than usual.' Then a friend said to him: 'Everyone feels like that. It's the best thing about a party.' 'This shared solitude,' he clarifies, 'can be seen, but it can also be heard.'

*

It wasn't yet high summer in Bern, but the sun was blazing. The city was swarming with crowds drawn by multiple and discrete activities when we arrived, after crossing an astonishingly calm, clean and silent quarter, in front of the Kunsthalle. My three-year-old son and I would be in the Swiss capital for several days and, as on every occasion when I found myself in Bern, visiting the Kunsthalle seemed to me an obligatory pleasure. But even though it was already late morning, we found the doors shut. We went to the bar in front of the building and I asked the waitresses behind the counter if they knew what time the exhibition would open, but they seemed unconcerned by the artistic life of the area. I learned, however, that a private view had been held there the previous evening. They weren't sure of the Kunsthalle's opening hours either, but said that it definitely wouldn't be open until later in the day, until 'two or three in the afternoon, maybe.' That was a surprise, because I had made sure to check the hours beforehand. Half-full beer steins left in front of the doors confirmed that the previous night had been a late one. We walked around the Kunsthalle to find out whether it might still be possible to see the Ivana Franke exhibition *Twilight: Neither perception nor non-perception*, soberly advertised by two invitation cards affixed to the large wooden doors. On them was an enigmatic poem by the artist Lantian Xie, which seemed to be a series of instructions and descriptions of spaces, works of art, actions and visions: 'Draw a small total dark ready to move … A black hole assembled, then disassembled, packed, shipped, unpacked, then reassembled again, lockstep with many signals buoyed somewhere 18 degrees beyond event's horizon.' Disappointed to find out that we might not be able to see Franke's exhibition, I decided to dial the Kunsthalle's number. After a few rings, a voice responded: 'Hello?' I explained to the voice, first in stumbling German and then in better English, that my son and I were in front of the building but that it seemed to be closed. 'No, we're absolutely open,' replied the voice calmly, in perfect French. 'I'm actually standing right behind the doors. We decided to keep them closed because the exhibition is meant to be viewed in darkness.' Then the doors opened and a smiling woman greeted us. She quickly guided us towards the exhibition space, briefing us on the visit and particularly on the parts of the Kunsthalle which were in total darkness: 'Don't worry. Leave your things in the cloakroom. Carry your child. There's a young man in the exhibition space. He'll never be far from you, but you won't see him at first. He'll call out to guide you.' Without a word, we passed through a thick black curtain and advanced towards the exhibition.

*

'The potential to think,' Agamben writes, 'experiencing itself and being capable of itself as potential not to think, makes itself into the trace of its own formlessness, a trace that no one has traced – pure matter.' This refers to a 'passion [of] impotentiality'. This capacity, like Charles Ray's cube of ink, is not a matter for thought but the matter of thoughts. An intelligible matter. A matter which itself, in one sense, thinks me. It is, once again, like seeing in the dark, 'the faculty of sensation…

[which] can sense its own lack of sensation, its own potentiality … pure taking-place.' A silence, pure matter of possibility.

*

Eyes wide in the dark, I was searching for any point of reference to find my bearings within the Kunsthalle. I had thought I knew it inside out. I could see nothing or, strictly speaking, almost nothing. In front of me was something that looked like a small, coloured LED light, and that seemed to be the only visual stimulus. My son clung to me. While I was feeling a little lost, not knowing what to do with my body, my eyes useless, a young man's voice – gentle and deliberately reassuring – came from somewhere in the middle of the room: 'You can follow the wall to your right. Put your hand out a few centimetres and you'll feel it. Follow me if you would, and I'll guide you to a room where the light from one of the pieces will help your eyes get used to the light level. I can give you my hand if you like.' I let myself be guided towards a space in which I saw a small coloured light with a slight glow. 'It will take a little while, perhaps five to seven minutes, for you to be able to see anything.' I asked if we could sit on the floor. The young man's voice said that we could.

'Look towards this little orange light. I'll describe the position and the shape of the sculpture here. You're about a metre away from it. You won't be able to see it yet. That's normal. You'll see that it's spherical. It comes out to about here,' he clarified, gesturing with a hand whose position I could only intuit. 'I'm not far away if you need me.' Sitting on the dark carpet, my son and I plunged our eyes into the unknown. I had the impression that our visual organs were stretching, growing, becoming something like antennae, straining to perceive anything in this space with its uncertain limits which seemed, suddenly, immense and unfamiliar. I imagined us as two animals huddled together, like those soft little mammals with outsized eyes and cold, humanlike paws which used to fascinate me in the nocturnal section of the zoo where my parents took me when I was a child.

*

According to Agamben, the scribe who dips his pen in thought inks it in 'its own formlessness'. To understand the nature of this thought, the philosopher returns to the example of 'the eye [in the dark which] does not see anything,' but which melds, 'has become in some way identical' with the darkness. This darkness – lack of definition, 'formlessness' –

could, in this way, be conceived not as an absence of form, but as something which is, for the eye, 'a base capable of receiving any colour.'

*

A few years after *Ink Box*, Charles Ray made a self-portrait. It is a life-sized framed colour photograph which shows the artist just after he had taken a dose of LSD. It is 1990. Ray, photographed from the front, is wearing a striped shirt and tortoiseshell glasses. His hair is longish, just slightly untidy. The artist presents himself as a rather conventional person; a serious, cerebral white man. When you look more closely, the half-closed eyes, the knitted brow, the slightly open mouth give the image a dreamlike quality, reinforced by the side lighting which lends the artist's body a peculiar glow. The strangeness of this photograph lies in our relationship with this body which, although it is there in front of us, seems at the same time to be fading out, becoming fluid, even evaporating. You almost feel a sense of lift, as though Ray were levitating within the photographic frame, floating in space as the shutter fell, saying to himself '*Yes*' – the title of the piece.

*

'The raucous, anarchic, noisy, variegated, tiger-striped, zebra-streaked, jumbled-up, mixed-up multiple, criss-crossed by myriad colours and myriad shades, is possibility itself … It is not potential, it is the very reverse of power, rather it is capaciousness. This noise is the opening.' The noise of the sea, the swell, absolute noise, the deafening noise of all noises are the 'perceived things born of these apperceptions.' Here, the neutral – the intense, scintillating, iridescent grey of Celmins' drawings – crystallises background noise and its violence; silence and the unspeakable emotions which are stifled, and yet still present in every one of the thousands of graphite strokes. '*Grey deep where breathes the breeze, all sleep. In the plain is born a noise. It is the breath of the night*,' concludes Serres. The chapter ends with a vision which leads me to understand that a noise, a cry, a hatred which I had not perceived, all reside in this silence.

*

Octavia E. Butler picked up on something when she wrote 'Speech Sounds'. In this 1983 short story, Butler describes a day in the life of Valerie Rye, a woman trying to survive in a post-apocalyptic world. People have lost the ability to speak. Almost all societal structures seem to have collapsed. Subjected to violence, predation and raiding, the wordless human beings communicate only through howls, sighs and grunts. '"Speech Sounds" was conceived in weariness, depression, and sorrow,' Butler recounts in her epilogue. It all started when she was taking the bus to visit a friend who was hospitalised and not expected to recover. One day, she witnessed a scene of astonishing violence. In the moment, nobody – including her – seemed to be able to hear, communicate or act, as though trapped in a state of paralysis and isolation. It was then that she decided on the first line of a new short story: 'There was trouble aboard the Washington Boulevard bus.'

*

In the kitchen of our vast rented house in Brussels, we spent a whole evening taking turns reading aloud from Paul B. Preciado's article 'Les Leçons du virus' (Learning from the Virus). All at once, what we were experiencing made sense – and it made us afraid. Preciado's writing is unforgiving and incisive. It insists on the need to expand the question of lockdowns to include biopolitical factors that go beyond DIY projects, the 'soft prison of our interiors' and our closed borders. 'European … societies have decided to construct themselves like entirely immunised communities,' he writes. 'Now we are living in detention centres in our own homes,' for 'the new necropolitical frontier has shifted from the coast of Greece toward the door of your home.' The text shudders with emotion and rage. Sorrow overflows theory. It is like a long chant that feels as though it were written urgently, in response to the needs of the moment. As if the pieces of a political puzzle were being assembled before our eyes. 'Lesbos now starts at your doorstep. And the border is forever tightening around you, pushing you ever closer to your body.' It was the first time that an essay on our current situation had moved us, putting words – words we spoke together as the night fell – to something that seemed always to have been there. 'Calais blows up in your face. The new frontier is the mask.' Or was it the opposite? What we were experiencing had to be truly experienced in order to be understood and mentally processed. 'The air that you breathe has to be yours alone. The new frontier is your epidermis. The new Lampedusa is your skin.'

*

It took longer than I expected. The young man in the dark was right. After several minutes which felt like an eternity, I began to make out shapes.

Ivana Franke's pieces gradually appeared. The other people who had been there all the time, invisible in the dark, came into view little by little. We were in the world of reflected lights, of 'highlights', out of the flow, the speed and the hurry of our everyday lives. The first sculpture, modestly sized, allowed us to discover the unsuspected powers of human sight, not only because of the myriad of details which revealed themselves or the depth of the landscape that appeared little by little, but because of how long this process of revelation went on. It was a sort of translucid sphere studded with points of light and served as an *amuse-bouche* for the following pieces, which were all like multiple variations on the same mysterious technical invention. The young male voice came again, inviting us to explore: 'Can you see better now? You're perfectly safe here. Do you see where this point of light is? It's at the centre of the room, and you can walk right up to it. Don't worry, there's nothing in the way of your path through the exhibition.' I took my son back into my arms and stood up. He said nothing, and neither did I. He must have been just as captivated as I was. Composed of a series of screen-like panels, the installations seemed to capture the light in three-dimensional line drawings; iridescent, almost imperceptible ever-shifting geometries. They reminded me of immense, crepuscular spider's webs vibrating at an unknown frequency, and at the same time of celestial bodies at such a distance that it was impossible to feel the immense, cosmic power of their movement. In what I thought was the third and final room of the exhibition, an immense moving structure like a vestige of some future architecture loomed out of the black void. As we looked up towards these forms and their dark angles, the young man asked if we would like to know the secret method the artist had used for these pieces. I hesitated for a moment, then agreed. He told us that he had spent a long time watching carefully to try to understand how Ivana Franke had come up with this magic trick resembling moving constellations. 'The artist strung nylon monofilament onto steel constructions. The specific patterns create geometric motifs which are only visible when light passes through them and a mechanism puts them in motion.' I didn't know what to say. Since we had entered the room, I had been oscillating between ecstasy and melancholy. I was close to bursting into tears, submerged by the feelings these evanescent reflections awoke in me. As we walked towards the exit, it struck me that no image, no photograph would be able to capture their subtlety and power. And yet they still existed in the eyes of the people immersing themselves in the darkness of the exhibition space, and in their nervous systems, and in their innermost selves. Almost reluctantly, dazzled, we went back out through the black curtain, towards the sun.

*

When we arrived at the cemetery, I remember being chilled to the bone by the realisation that we were the only ones there. It was just the three of us: my sister, our mother and me, exactly like in that night-time photograph. Only older, drawn, a few decades on. And you had disappeared from the picture. We were standing looking at the ground, and uniformed men were lined up on one side, not saying a word, rifles held across their torsos. A storm was threatening. The sky was grey; my body was trembling. I looked up and held the urn in my gaze, wondering how much it weighed. Nobody wanted to say anything, so nothing was said. In any case, I would have heard nothing but the gunshots ringing through the sky as the tears streamed down my cheeks, my heart pierced – like a raincloud – by the sudden, sharp reports. If I regret anything, it's that I wasn't able to see you, to see your body and your face before they went into the flames visible through a large window a little way away, behind the industrial tiles and the dull monochrome doors. I wouldn't have imagined that such a place would so strongly resemble part of a hospital, somewhere between the operating room and the storeroom. Only the signage reminded us where we really were. In a crematorium, the management of stock and bodies is achieved by a single operation: reducing them to ashes. There isn't much in the way of ritual or religion. I wasn't prepared. When it was our turn, we went in. My mother said to me, very fast, 'You don't have to look.' I was so filled with emotion that I felt as though I were floating, moving through space like my own ghost. A few seconds later, the heavy wooden box was on the conveyer belt, on its way to pass ineluctably through the fire. You were sinking into another universe. I wanted to make it all stop but it was too late. I wanted to shout, 'Wait, I've changed my mind!' I want to see you, to lean over your body. I want my tears to fall onto your forehead and flood your face, running through the channels of your wrinkles. I want to grasp your large, round shoulders, to feel the temperature of your chest against mine and to understand, really understand, skin to skin, what death is, what your death is. To really feel it. To touch it. Is that why you came back the other day, in the kitchen, after all? So that I could do something I had never done when you were alive and hold you in my arms? Or was it to tell me that you knew, knew that you hadn't seen me that day, just as you weren't there at the births of my daughters, the birth of my son? There's a part of you in them: their clear gazes, the lines of their bodies, their strength, their gentleness, their courage. I turned my back on you once, twice, again, until that day when your bones, your skin, your hair went up in smoke. But you are there every day, in everything I do, when I hang a painting, when I dig the garden, when I chop a vegetable in the kitchen or walk through dead leaves. I fled, but there you are in spite of me. You are in my fingers, in my eyes which never touched you, but which see you and write you now.

*

The solitude of lockdown can become everything or nothing. It is not simply an inconvenience; it can become an instrument by which to advance in a certain understanding, to sharpen our awareness, like the process Thiellement refers to as 'black work', the first phase of the alchemical process to transform lead into gold. What the present demands of us, he says, 'is to take this horrible lockdown and turn it into a *marvel*.'

*

A few months ago, I realised that I had accumulated quite a large number of resignation letters. These letters, begun in moments of rage when I felt the urgent need to give it all up, had, however, mostly stayed as rough drafts. In the meantime, I had in fact left all my jobs – teaching, museum positions, and so on – to create a void which seemed necessary to me, although I didn't know exactly what I was going to do with it. I had written all these letters, sometimes long, often furious. And then I had filed them away unsent once the anger had passed, once reason must have regained the upper hand. Only a few weeks later, I read Charles Reeve's article on what he called 'the great resignation' in the United States, which he explains in the context of the COVID-19 outbreak: thousands of people, who were seemingly neither victims of workplace harassment nor facing unbearable situations, resigned *en masse*, refused to go on. And there sat my letters, like a multi-year archive preserving all my abortive or adjourned attempts to say 'no'. Instead I continued to say 'yes' most of the time, or to say nothing at all. To keep quiet. At the end of that long series of letters, once I had read them all and laid them end to end, I thought to myself that the final letter to write should be one addressed to you. I still don't know why. The strange thing is that the last time we met, we couldn't talk to each other at all. We were content just to see each other. The illness had damaged your brain to such an extent that there was only one word you could still say: 'yes'. You repeated it incessantly, punctuating our lacunary conversation with a 'yes' for any and every question I asked you, 'yes' for every action, 'yes' for everything that you wanted to show me. I remember the agitation all around us, patients getting worked up and shouting only metres from where we sat. A carer who had noticed how upset I was came over to me and said that you were experiencing the world in the same way as a two-year-old child. I still wonder what that 'yes' meant – the last word you could or would say, like a relic or a ruin of language which still remains floating within my memory, echoing. I realise that the first words I wrote to you came after that series of letters in which I tried to say 'no'. Perhaps you had been trying to send me a message. A message I never received.

*

One day, Thiellement decided to disappear completely from all forms of social media. In October 2020, he published an article on his website entitled 'Le Livre sans visage, ou : pourquoi je quitte les réseaux sociaux' (Book Without a Face, or, Why I'm

Leaving Social Media). I got the news of his retreat from the digital world in a message which he had sent to his contacts. Almost immediately, I read his manifesto and found it beautiful, humble and sincere. And interesting, because at one time Thiellement's life and work had been indissociable from his use of Facebook. It was a 'Bible', he writes, in which he participated 'almost without limits, whether it was for personal or professional ends, active or contemplative, for exchanges of information or self-promotion, for research or networking.' I understood that this farewell letter was also at once an analysis and a self-exegesis. The lucid, determined criticism of a belief in the necessity of being present. A chronicle of the fatigue of distortion. 'I'm not leaving the stage, I'm going to another theatre.' *Le Livre sans visage* was also the name of Thiellement's online journal, where he related his thoughts and his projects. For him, the lockdown would prove to be the object of a mutation, a revelation and an entry into shadow, towards a smaller place where 'we can talk in low voices … lock the doors and dance 'til dawn.' Emily Dickinson wrote in 1873: 'But Silence is Infinity. Himself have not a face.' These lines feature on a torn piece of envelope, one of Dickinson's habitual writing surfaces. She took full advantage of the varied geometries afforded by the medium and of the marks left on the paper once it had been folded, unfolded, cut, refolded. Several dozen of these envelope poems are reproduced in facsimile in *The Gorgeous Nothings*, edited by Jen Bervin and Marta Werner. Bervin, herself a poet and artist, explains that the re-use of scraps and scattered remainders of texts was foundational to Dickinson's work, for the poet always kept several of her short texts on her person, folded up in her pockets, along with a pencil. The fact that she worked in pencil is not a coincidence. As with Vija Celmins' work, graphite is a representation of density and equally of the material's fragility, its brittleness. Strength, depth. Vulnerability. It is blackness, night, secrecy. It is also the fluidity of swift thought, the living impermanence of poetry written in secret, by hand and in the margins. Flowing emotion like seawater, which rises to the surface and floods the page in Celmins' work, also inundates the reverse sides, the folds, the bits and pieces of commercial stationery in Dickinson's poetry. Graphite is in keeping with the writer's silence, with her confined life, for she lived – as the novelist Dominique Fortier reminds us – in the isolation of her own home, reluctant first to go beyond her garden and then to leave her house at all. In the end, Dickinson spent the last years of her life shut up in her bedroom. In contrast to the studies which have dealt with the poet's silence, Fortier does not believe that this confinement was merely something that Dickinson had to endure. It was also 'the sign of a liberty which grew progressively more extensive and more assured.' Although Dickinson has often been described as a reclusive poet who did not wish to be published, Bervin reminds us in her introduction to *The Gorgeous Nothings* that the poet produced more than 3,000 textual compositions including poems, drafts of poems, letters and fragments of prose. A major and constellational epistolary art on the backs of postcards, pieces of notepaper and envelopes, sent through the post to a myriad of correspondents. This infinite, invisible silence makes us afraid. It may be mysterious to us, but it is necessary, now more than ever. Thiellement, who rightly admits that he had the advantage of being well-known before he disappeared from social media, has in his own way also committed to a state of being unknown. He has silenced himself. 'Since I made this decision,' he writes, 'I feel like I've started living, finally living.'

*

Only weeks after Thiellement announced his retreat, Preciado was interviewed for *Vogue Hommes* and proposed a kind of discipline to readers, saying in essence that they should try to give up alcohol, coffee and social media. I see this as a very practical, if surprising, invitation. He gives us to understand that by doing this you will see your body transform little by little, you will act in a different way, and you will develop new skills. Reading this claim again, I think he may have been thinking of writing a survival guide. Such crises are older than the one we have lately been living through.

*

Octavia E. Butler heard 'the illness and the silence' before they spread over the world. What is fascinating in 'Speech Sounds' is the soundscape itself. Its silence is the opposite of an absence of noise. Everything is void, shouts and chaos. We don't know whether humans have lost their voices or whether they have lost the use of words, of speech. They defend themselves; they communicate with brusque gestures. In haste and anger they show each other things without really knowing whether they are being understood. Bodies hit, rub, scratch. Mouths groan, howl. Emotions are expressed only through sighs, gasps, breaths, of fear or abandon. Gazes are silent. Valerie Rye thinks at one point that she will never hear her own name spoken again, until – on her tragic journey, amid the disaster – she meets two children who seem to have something different in their eyes… Michel Serres also saw this silence, as hateful as 'the breath of the night.' The vision is sombre, chilling, apocalyptic. The imperceptible, threatening *Genesis* of the end. Hatred begins in obscurity, in the void and the fear of the night, in a breeze, a breath, a whistling which becomes a murmur, an explosion, an invisible and destructive rage. Preciado, meanwhile, describes a kind of ethics of obscurity. For him, only in confronting silence with another silence can something new be formed. In this retreat, our brains will see things differently, do different things. Our destinies will come together in a new way.

*

I am thinking about something like an ethics of obscurity. A listening position which would oppose another silence to the silence which is imposed. I plunge in, I embrace this retreat. There my body, all at once, develops new skills; my brain begins to perceive unknown things. Our destinies come together in a new way.

*

Brussels, at the end of the month of April. I planned to show an image. Just one. In fact it isn't an image but a text, a piece of text, a fragment. For the last few weeks, as it happened, I hadn't shown any images at all. I had proposed to work in another way. As was my habit, I arrived slightly early to make sure I would have enough time. Time to go through reception, to tuck the audio-visual equipment I needed for the class under my arm, then to walk through the corridors of the school and climb half a storey and to install, in silence, the framework of our conversations. To wait for the whole group to arrive and for the discussions to begin. I had named this project Ø. It was an experiment which I conceived of as something almost scientific; nameless, designated only by the mathematical symbol which signifies an empty set. It was a seminar 'about nothing', as I had put it in the mandatory description. This was a principle which I had already practised elsewhere and which I had planned to take on anew, collectively. At first, we hadn't said anything. Then, from the long silences which punctuated our exchanges, something came into being: what it was we were going to talk about, and how we were going to talk about it. We tried to capture what was emerging from these voids, from our embarrassment. It was as if this particular silence insisted that we discuss, that we act, or that we simply experience its weight, its hardness, its transparency and its opacity. As if we were managing from time to time to extract something, the very matter in which we were caught or sometimes absorbed, and to hold it floating before us within arm's reach, rotating it for observation. Trying to maintain this space, I constantly restrained myself from the game I was so used to – filling the void. It was beautiful but difficult. And so I had planned to show only one image. It was just behind me, on my left, on the wall of this light, empty room whose low ceiling was patterned with large metal pipes. As usual, I sent a message to the group to let them know I had arrived, reminding them of the room and the time of the seminar. I was not then aware that this email would be the last teaching communication I would write for a long time. When my message received no response, I went and stood in the middle of the room, halfway to the door, exactly where the group usually sat for our discussions. As if to preserve a record of that moment, I took a photograph. The room was empty, all the chairs vacant, the vast white wall, the black text projected onto it. I thought that there was something to this arrangement, that the picture I had taken could be that of a conference yet to start or of a seminar that had just ended. It was evidence of what was happening; that is to say, nothing. Then I left the school and, dazzled by the sudden, brutal brightness, deafened by the noisy road, I crossed the large avenue which leads down towards the park and began to walk at random through the streets. I wondered what I was going to do, but it wasn't at all important. All of a sudden, my time was free. In my pocket, my mobile phone has stored in its memory an image where you see something that looks like a screen and these words, which I had just read in the news – and which I had thought would be a good starting point for my seminar – written by Paul B. Preciado: 'Let's turn off our mobile phones and disconnect from the internet. Let's start a great blackout in defiance of the satellites observing us and reflect together on the revolution to come.'

*

I have just realised that this letter is the first I have ever written to you. From you, I remember only short messages, written on the thick, shiny paper of a greetings card or on a modest, folded note slipped into an envelope for me on special occasions. I remember your handwriting exactly: careful, round, solid. You often asked me to explain some rule of spelling or grammar to you. Your writing had formed alongside you, shaped by a life of manual labour which, unlike mine, did not often require the use of words. I couldn't say why those few phrases, written with careful concentration, are still fixed in my memory. They move me because they represent the rare traces of your attention and because they reflect, behind their economy of means, what I imagine to be your feelings. But I realise now that they were never able to mask the vulnerability on which they were founded. That of a grown man who was trying to express himself as clearly as possible, as if he always felt judged by some invisible force. As if I were catching sight of a ghost of you in your youth, a boy about to spend the tail-end of his childhood chained to a machine, the same age that I was when I realised that my life could be something like an infinite stroll through a world made of libraries. But I wrote and rewrote these words an incalculable number of times before making up my mind to address them to you. I have taken a path so different from yours, but perhaps, in my own way, I share with you this feeling that something is lacking. It is part of my inheritance. I write to you not to fill this absence, but to continue to inhabit it. I write to you, but I know that you can't read it. Your silence belongs to us and was shared between us. I write to you, but I am speaking to this silence.

Notes

p.8
Brian Eno interviewed by Riz Khan on 'One on One', *Al Jazeera*, June 2011

pp.9–10
– David Toop, 'How Much World Do You Want?: Ambient Listening and Its Questions', in Monty Adkins and Simon Cummings (eds.), *Music Beyond Airports: Appraising Ambient Music*, Huddersfield, University of Huddersfield Press, 2019, pp.1–2, 19
– Richard Kostelanetz, *John Cage (ex)plain(ed)*, New York, Schirmer Books, 1996, p.121

pp.11–12
Judy Nylon interviewed by Bart Plantenga, 'Live Now, Wise Up, Die Well: an Interview with Judy Nylon, Punk Legend', *3AM Magazine*, 2001

p.16
'Voices on Tape; Sounds from the Spirit World?' in Will Bradbury (ed.), *Into the Unknown*, Pleasantville, New York/Montreal, Reader's Digest Association Inc., 1981, pp. 198–99

pp.17–18
– Carl Michael von Hausswolf, assisted by M. S. C. Harding, '1485.0 KHZ: Friedrich Jürgenson and the Voices of the Dead', *Cabinet*, no. 1, *Invented Languages*, Winter 2000–2001
– David Toop, *Ocean of Sound: Aether Talk, Ambient Sound and Imaginary Worlds*, London, Serpent's Tail, 1995, p.270
– Robert Rauschenberg on the subject of his *White Paintings*,

published online on moma.org: https://www.moma.org/audio/playlist/40/639

p.21
La Monte Young, *Composition 1960 #2*, 1960

p.24
Mieko Shiomi, *Water Music*, instruction on the label of the eponymous edition, ReFlux Editions, New York, 1991

pp.25–27
Nina Power, 'Towards a Feminism of the Void', November 2017, published on the author's website: https://ninapower.net/2017/11/09/191/

p.28
Anna Raimondo interviewed by Yann Chateigné, *Hospitalité* [Hospitality] #2, Studio K, radio KANAL – Centre Pompidou, January 2021

p.29
Rebecca Solnit, 'A Short History of Silence', in *The Mother of All Questions: Further Feminisms*, London, Granta, 2017, p.17

pp.31, 36–37
Vija Celmins, in 'Chuck Close in Conversation with Vija Celmins About Her Dense Yet Infinite Drawings', *Artspace*, April 2017

p.36
Vija Celmins, in Calvin Tomkins, 'Vija Celmins's Surface Matters', *The New Yorker*, August 2019

p.41
– Alain Viala, 'Who's there : voir Watteau avec Pierre Michon' [Who's There: Seeing Watteau with Pierre Michon], *Les Dossiers du Grihl*, special issue no. 1, 2022

– Calvin Tomkins, ‘Meaning Machines: The Sculptures of Charles Ray’, *The New Yorker*, May 2015

p.42
Jean-Pierre Criqui, ‘Tric Trac pour Tony Smith’ [Trictrac for Tony Smith], in *Un trou dans la vie : Essais sur l’art depuis 1960* [A Hole in One’s Life: Essays on Art Post-1960], Paris, Desclée de Brouwer, 1960, p.41

pp.43, 49, 60–61, 74
Michel Serres, Geneviève James (trans.) and James Nielson (trans.), ‘La Belle Noiseuse’, in *Genesis*, Ann Arbor, University of Michigan Press, 1995, pp.12–15, 19, 22, 25–26

p.47
– Muriel Pic, ‘Orientation’ [Orientation], in *Élegies documentaires* [Documentary Elegies], in the Opus incertum collection, Paris, Macula, 2016, p.59
– Don C. Talayesva, *Sun Chief: The Autobiography of a Hopi Indian*, London, Yale University Press, 2013

pp.50, 54–55, 68
Pacôme Thiellement and Delphine Dora interviewed by Yann Chateigné, ‘After Hours: Confinés depuis la nuit des temps’ [After Hours: locked down since the dawn of time], Studio K, Radio Kanal – Centre Pompidou, January 2021

p.50
Delphine Dora ft. Pacôme Thiellement, ‘confinés depuis la nuit des temps’ [locked down since the dawn of time], from the album *un monde sans dehors / un dehors sans monde* [a world without an outside / an outside without a world], carton records, 2022

pp.53, 57, 59
Giorgio Agamben, Daniel Heller-Roazen (ed., trans), ‘Pardes: The

Writing of Potentiality', in *Potentialities: Collected Essays in Philosophy*, Stanford, Stanford University Press, 1999, pp.216–18

pp.54–55
René Daumal, David Coward (trans.) and E.A. Lovatt (trans.), *A Night of Serious Drinking*, in the Tusk Ivories collection, New York, Overlook Press, 2003, p.6

p.56
Lantan Xie, 'Rounding Midnight', in Lantian Xie and Sabih Ahmed (eds.), *Mass Traffic*, Milan, Mousse Publishing, 2023

pp.61–62, 73
Octavia E. Butler, 'Speech Sounds', in *Bloodchild and Other Stories*, New York, Seven Stories Press, 2005, pp.89, 97, 109

p.62, 77
Paul B. Preciado, 'Biosurveillance : sortir de la prison molle de nos intérieurs' [Biosurveillance: escaping the soft prison of our interiors], *Mediapart*, April 2020

pp.62–63
– Paul B. Preciado, Molly Stevens (trans.), 'Learning from the Virus', *Artforum*, May/June 2020
– Bilge Sayim and Ivana Franke, 'Towards a Phenomenology of the Unknown', in *Retreat into Darkness: Towards a Phenomenology of the Unknown*, Berlin/Leipzig, Ernst Schering Foundation and Spector Books, 2018, p.109

p.68
Charles Reeve, 'Le Covid et "la grande démission"' [COVID and the 'great resignation'], *Lundimatin*, no. 304, September 2021

pp.70–71
– Pacôme Thiellement, 'Le livre sans visage, ou : pourquoi je quitte

les réseaux sociaux' [Book Without a Face, or, Why I'm Leaving Social Media], October 2020, published on the author's website: http://www.pacomethiellement.com/corpus_texte.php?id=474_
– Emily Dickinson, Amherst Manuscript # 348 – 'Silence is all we dread', Amherst College, Amhurst MA, available online at http://edickinson.org/
– Marta Werner and Jen Bervin (eds.), *Emily Dickinson: The Gorgeous Nothings*, New York, Granary Books, 2012

p.72
– Dominique Fortier interviewed by Marie Richeux, 'Emily Dickinson m'a appris les vertus du regard lent et vrai sur les choses' [Emily Dickinson taught me the value of a slow and genuine perspective on things], on 'Par les temps qui courent' [These Days], *France Culture*, December 2020
– Jen Bervin, 'Studies in Scale: An Introduction', in *Emily Dickinson: The Gorgeous Nothings*, op. cit., p.8
– Interview of Pacôme Thiellement by Christian Rosset, 'Laisser des espaces ouverts est indispensable à la vie' [Leaving open spaces is essential to life], *Diacritik*, October 2021

p.73
Paul B. Preciado interviewed by Nelly Kaprièlian, 'In the Mood to Change the World', *Vogue Hommes*, Autumn–Winter 2020-2021

The author wishes to thank Véronique Bacchetta, Gabe Beckhurst Feijoo, Caroline Dumalin, Jean-Pierre Greff, Charlotte Herzig, Isabelle Manci, Annie Serrati, Bernard Vischer & Antonella Notari, as well as all who, in their absence or presence, have accompanied the writing of this book. This publication has received financial support from the Shadow Foundation in Rolle, Switzerland.

Yann Chateigné Tytelman is an author and art curator living in Brussels. He has been curator at the KANAL–Centre Pompidou Brussels, head of the Visual Arts Department at HEAD – Geneva, and chief curator at CAPC in Bordeaux, among other positions. He is a guest lecturer in the Curatorial Studies programme at KASK & Conservatorium, Gent. In 2023, he co-founded Celador, an art space run by a reading group collective, in Brussels.

Clem Clement is a literary translator and an editor whose published work includes a chapter of *Chicanes* by Clara Schulmann.

Also published by Les Fugitives

In 'the quick brown fox' collection:

Harriet Armstrong
To Rest Our Minds and Bodies

Charlotte Beeston
The White Flower

Penelope Curtis
After Nora

Erica van Horn
We Still Have the Telephone

Michèle Roberts
French Cooking for One

Kyra Wilder
Gloss

Lauren Elkin
No. 91/92: notes on a Parisian commute

In translation from French:

Catherine Axelrad
Célina
trans. Philip Terry

Jeanne Benameur
The Child Who
trans. Bill Johnston

Ananda Devi
Eve out of Her Ruins
The Living Days
trans. Jeffrey Zuckerman

Colette Fellous
This Tilting World
trans. Sophie Lewis

Jean Frémon
Now, Now, Louison
Nativity, trans. Cole Swensen
Portrait Tales, trans. John Taylor

Mireille Gansel
Translation as Transhumance
trans. Ros Schwartz

Maylis de Kerangal
Eastbound
trans. Jessica Moore

Julia Kerninon
A Respectable Occupation
trans. Ruth Diver

Camille Laurens
Little Dancer Aged Fourteen
trans. Willard Wood

Noémi Lefebvre
Blue Self-Portrait
Poetics of Work
trans. Sophie Lewis

Nathalie Léger
Suite for Barbara Loden
trans. Natasha Lehrer
Exposition
trans. Amanda DeMarco
The White Dress
trans. Natasha Lehrer

Emilienne Malfatto
May the Tigris Grieve for You
trans. Lorna Scott Fox

Lucie Paye
Absence
trans. Natasha Lehrer

Shumona Sinha
Down with the Poor!
trans. Teresa Lavender Fagan

Jérôme Prieur
Zombie Proust
trans. Nancy Kline

Clara Schulmann
Chicanes, trans. Clem Clement, Ruth Diver, Lauren Elkin, *et al.*

Anne Serre
The Governesses
The Fool and Other Moral Tales
trans. Mark Hutchinson

Sylvie Weil
Selfies
trans. Ros Schwartz